Gadchick Presents

A Beginner's Guide to iPhone 6 and iPhone 6 Plus

(Or iPhone 4s, iPhone 5, iPhone 5c, iPhone 5s with iOS 8)

By Katie Morris

Putting the Geek in Chic

www.Gadchick.com

Cover Image © pkproject - Fotolia

Table of Contents

Introduction

The latest iPhone models were released on September 19th in the United States and the United Kingdom, and according to Apple, are the "biggest advancements in iPhone history." It's a clever play on words, as the new models both sport much larger screens than the iPhones of yesteryear. Whereas the iPhone 4S and below had a meager 3.5 inch screen (considered generous at the time), the iPhone 5, 5S and 5C were stretched out to 4 inches. Faced with stiff competition from Android flagships that have long featured big screens, the iPhone 6 and 6 Plus are Apple's authoritative answer to the growing number of iOS fans restlessly awaiting their own big phones. The new phones are powered behind the scenes by Apple's latest software release, iOS 8, which also brings many features and changes with it.

This guide is designed to walk you through the most important parts of the phone, from the basics and learning how to navigate through the phone, to more advanced features like setting up email accounts and understanding what the cloud really is. Towards the end, a list of the 20 top paid and free applications will be available to add many different functionalities to your phone once you are comfortable enough with it.

Chapter 1: Overview of Basic Features

The two new iPhones come with many different features besides their size difference. Here is a basic overview of what each new model comes with, and how it compares to last year's iPhone 5S.

	iPhone 5S	iPhone 6	iPhone 6 Plus
Screen Size	4 inches	4.7 inches	5.5 inches
Resolution	1136 x 640	1134 x 750	1920 x 1080
Capacity	16, 32, & 64 GB	16, 64, & 128 GB	16, 64, & 128 GB
Colors	Space Gray, Silver, Gold	Space Gray, Silver, Gold	Space Gray, Silver, Gold
Camera	8 MP iSight with digital stabilization	8 MP iSight with digital stabilization	8 MP iSight with optical stabilization
Processor	A7 Chip with M7 motion coprocessor	A8 chip with M8 motion coprocessor and barometer	A8 chip with M8 coprocessor and barometer
NFC	No	Yes	Yes
Battery	Up to 10 hours talk time Up to 10 hours browsing time	Up to 14 hours talk time Up to 10 hours browsing time	Up to 24 hours talk time Up to 12 hours talk time
Network Speeds	LTE up to 100 Mbps	LTE up to 150 Mbps	LTE up to 150 Mbps

Main Differences between the iPhone 6 and 6 Plus

If you have not yet purchased the new iPhone but are torn between the two models, consider these points to help with your decision:

- While both models are much thinner and lighter than their predecessors, the iPhone 6 Plus is considerably larger than the 6. An in person side-by-side comparison is strongly encouraged so you can accurately see which size is more comfortable for you.

- Both new models are identical in design, but the 6 Plus does have some small improvements over the 6. The 6 Plus comes with optical image stabilization instead digital, extended battery life, and a full HD 1080p resolution. Finally, the 6 Plus will allow you to be more productive by laying out apps and presenting them to you in a way that's akin to the iPad and iPad mini.

- The iPhone 6 is certainly the more portable version of the two. If you usually wear pants with smaller pockets or want something with a bigger screen than the iPhone 5S while retaining easy one handed operation, the iPhone 6 will be ideal for you.

Chapter 2: Using the Phone

Sleep/Wake and Powering On/Off

For the first time in iPhone history, Apple has moved the Sleep/Wake button from the top edge of the phone to the right side in order to accommodate the larger screens and still make the power button accessible during one handed operation. After each use of the iPhone, be sure to press this button in order to lock the screen and prevent any accidental touches. Doing so ensures you preserve the battery life by keeping the screen off unless necessary. If a call, message, or notification comes through, the screen will light up again in order to show you what's going on. When you need to access your iPhone again, clicking the Sleep/Wake button and sliding to the right will open up the phone again, bringing you to the last screen you were on before it locked.

There is an Auto-Lock feature that automatically shuts the screen off for you if left untouched for too long. To change the settings to better suit your needs, simply go to Settings > General > Auto-Lock and select whichever timer works best for you.

If your iPhone 6 or 6 Plus is shut off, you can power your phone on by pressing and holding the Sleep/Wake button until you see the Apple logo appear. To shut your phone down completely, press and hold the Sleep/Wake button until you see a notification at the top, and simply swipe to the right to confirm.

Home Button

Perhaps one of the greatest attractions to the iPhone, aside from its beautiful and elegant design, is its simplicity. Unlike other phones on the market, the iPhone stands out as one of the simplest largely because the front is adorned by only one home button. There are no soft keys to accidentally press, and no other buttons to add confusion. The home button features several different shortcuts. No matter where you are in the phone, and regardless of what app you are using, simply click the home button once to be taken back to your home screen. This is great if you ever get lost in a sea of menus or need to quickly jump to the home screen in order to access a different application.

Press and hold the home button to enable Siri, Apple's beloved digital personal assistant. We will go over Siri in greater detail later on, but know that should you ever need help using the phone hands-free, Siri is a wonderful feature and an invaluable asset.

Another function we will cover soon is multitasking, which can be done by clicking the home button twice in rapid succession.

Phone Calls

The iPhone's simple design and ease of use is translated well into how it handles phone calls. To dial a number, just click on the green Phone icon on your home screen, and you will be greeted with a number pad. Type in the phone number, and press the green button to send the call through. When the call starts, you will be able to end the call by pressing the red button during connection or after the other end picks up.

Holding the phone up to your ear will activate the proximity sensor located at the top of your phone. This sensor's main purpose is to make sure that the screen shuts off when you put the phone up to your ear, to prevent your face from accidentally tapping buttons on the screen.

If someone calls you, you will be given the choice to either Decline or Accept the call. If you want to leave the call alone but needed to silence it, just press the Sleep/Wake button and the phone will stop ringing or vibrating.

To call someone that's already in your contact list, just tap on the contacts icon (middle one on the bottom row of icons), find and select the person or company you want to call, and tap the phone icon in their contact card to initiate the call.

Back in the Phone app, you will see a few more icons on the bottom toolbar: Favorites, Recents, and Voicemail.

Favorites is where you can find contacts that you've designated as important in one area. If you have numbers you find yourself frequently dialing, the Favorites tab is a great place to store them so you don't have to hunt them down in the contact list each time you need to make a phone call. To add a favorite contact, click on Favorites and then the + button, or you can find that person's contact card through Contacts, click on it, and select Add to Favorites.

Recents is where you will find the call logs. You can sort it by either all calls or just missed calls by tapping on the appropriate button at the top. If you are viewing all calls, the red ones will indicate missed calls. To delete an entry, swipe left and tap on the red Delete button.

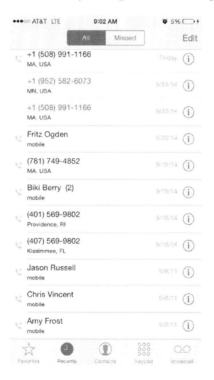

Lastly, the Voicemail icon on the toolbar will take you to your voicemail inbox. If you do not have Visual Voicemail, your phone will make a call to your inbox where you can listen to your messages and follow the prompts to save or delete them. If you do have Visual Voicemail, you will be able to view all of your voicemails on one screen and instead of having to listen to everything just to get to one message, you can tap on the voicemail you'd like to play back. As with Recents, you can delete a voicemail by swiping from left to right and pressing the red button.

Adding Contacts

There are a few ways to add contacts to your phone. If you already know the prospective contact's phone number, go to Phone > Keypad and type in the phone number. When you're finished, press Add to Contacts. It will ask you to either create a new contact, or add to existing if it's a new number associated with a contact that's already stored in the phone.

Another way to add a contact is if you go to Phone > Recents, and click on the information icon next to the phone number - it looks like an "I" with a blue circle around it. Just like the first method, here you will be given the option to either create a new contact or add to existing contact. To delete contacts, go to Phone > Contacts or tap the Contacts icon on your home screen. Scroll through the contact list until you find the contact you wish to remove, then swipe from right to left and tap the Delete button.

Do Not Disturb

If you don't want to be interrupted with a phone call, for example during sleep or an important meeting, you can enable Do Not Disturb on the iPhone. This will send calls straight to voicemail and only allow calls from your Favorites to come in. To enable Do Not Disturb, either swipe up from the bottom of the screen to bring up the control center and tap the crescent moon icon, or go to Settings > Do Not Disturb and turn it on.

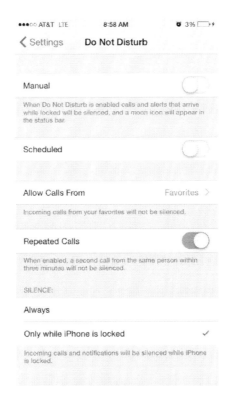

You can customize how Do Not Disturb works by configuring many different things in the menu. If you fall asleep around the same time every night and do not want to be disturbed, you can assign specific hours of the day that your phone automatically switches to Do Not Disturb mode. You can also disable calls from everyone including Favorites, or enable calls to come through if a call is made two or more times in case of emergencies.

Bluetooth

Bluetooth is a wireless technology that allows your iPhone to connect with other Bluetooth-capable devices within 200 feet, but most Bluetooth devices are only made to work within a smaller radius, around 30 to 40 feet. Bluetooth is useful because it allows you to create strong, stable connections with other devices without using any data. If you are using a Bluetooth headset or keyboard, for example, you can use it as long as you'd like without worrying about consuming data.

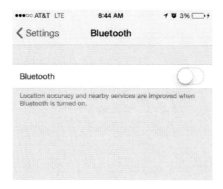

To turn Bluetooth on, go to Settings > Bluetooth. Once the other Bluetooth device is in pairing mode (consult that product's manual for instructions) you will see the name appear under the Devices list. Tap on the device name and follow the onscreen prompts to connect.

Wi-Fi

Unless you are on an unlimited data plan, most network providers offer a limited amount of data that you can use every month. It's important to know exactly how much data is allocated for your phone line so that you can avoid paying extra charges. A great way to enjoy your iPhone without worrying about going over the data limit is by connecting it to a Wi-Fi network.

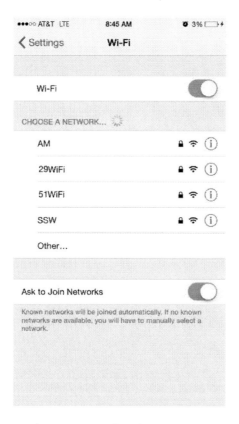

Wi-Fi networks are essentially wireless networks that are limited to a certain range, usually between 40 to 60 feet. Your phone can connect to Wi-Fi network access points (better known as "hotspots") in order to reduce the amount of data you use. Anytime the iPhone is connected to a Wi-Fi hotspot, you are not using any data since its uploading and downloading information through a separate frequency. Hotspots can be found all over, including coffee shops, restaurants, car dealers, Laundromats, retail stores, and gyms. If you have an internet provider at home, you more than likely have a wireless network in your home as well. Contact your internet service provider (ISP) for more information on your existing service and how to connect to your home network.

To connect the iPhone to a Wi-Fi network, tap the Settings icon on your home screen and select Wi-Fi near the top. You may have noticed that there was also a toggle on and off button. This should always be on if you are not on an unlimited data plan so that you may connect automatically to saved networks. You can also turn Wi-Fi on or off by swiping up from the bottom of the screen to open the Control Center and toggling the Wi-Fi icon in the top left corner.

Going back to the Wi-Fi menu, the phone will scan and display the available wireless networks around you. If that network has a password, you will see a lock icon next to it signifying that it's secure. If there is no lock icon, the network is completely open and anyone can join. If possible, refrain from using wide open networks to load sensitive data such as a bank website since it can leave you open for hackers.

At the bottom of the Wi-Fi settings screen you will see one more toggle option titled "Ask to Join Networks". This option will notify you of open and available networks instead of just automatically connecting to them, and should be left on as a security precaution.

Personal Hotspot

Not only can your iPhone connect to Wi-Fi hotspots, but it can turn itself into a Wi-Fi hotspot as well. Turning your phone into a personal hotspot lets you connect other devices to the web (like a laptop or a Wi-Fi only iPad) when there aren't any other reliable Wi-Fi networks available. Like normal hotspots, your range will also be between 40 to 60 feet. The hotspot feature is not available on all carriers, and some service plans may charge extra for this feature so check with your provider before using it.

To turn on your iPhone's hotspot feature, tap on Settings > Personal Hotspot. Toggle it on, and on the device you want to connect, search for your iPhone in the list of Wi-Fi networks and type in the password shown on the hotspot menu. By default the iPhone hotspot is set up with a secure, complicated password. You can change the password if you wish by clicking on Wi-Fi Password in the hotspot menu and creating a new password of at least 8 characters. When complete, you will see a blue line across the top of the screen indicating the connection was a success.

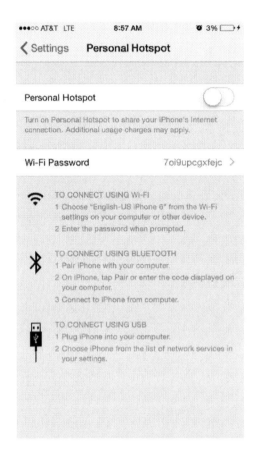

If you have a device that does not have a built in wireless network adapter, you can hardwire it by connecting your iPhone to that device using your sync cable and selecting the iPhone network.

Reachability

Like many of the other new iOS 8 features, this one was built with the larger screens in mind. To enable reachability, quickly and lightly tap (don't click!) on the home button twice. You will notice that the top half of the screen slides down to the bottom half, essentially allowing you to reach the top parts of the screen with your thumb, without overextending yourself.

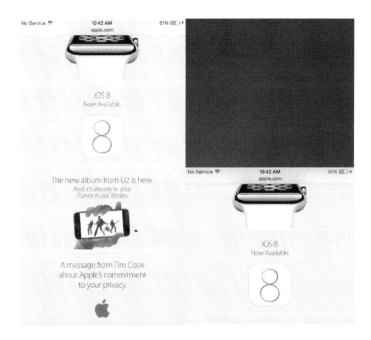

You may not need to use it on the iPhone 6, but iPhone 6 Plus owners may find themselves using this handy feature quite often. If you'd prefer to have reachability disabled, you have the option to disable it by going to Settings > General > Accessibility > Reachability.

Typing

Fans have been eagerly awaiting one of the most anticipated additions to the iPhone - third party keyboards. You can now download a host of keyboards and add-ons that better suit your typing needs, including Swype, Swift Key, and a newcomer called PopKey that allows you to easily send text messages using animated "reaction" gifs for those moments where a picture gets the point across much better than words.

The stock iOS 8 keyboard has received some updates as well. Most notable is the predictive text feature that learns your speech patterns and behaviors. This predictive text is unique in that it can distinguish between different people and how you talk to them. For example, if you regularly text your loved one "I'm coming home now, I love you" before you leave work, it will give you that option for autocomplete, but not if you were having a conversation with your boss.

Another cool feature on the new iOS 8 keyboard is its ability to provide you with quick responses when faced with a choice. Imagine a friend texted you which flavor of ice cream you would prefer; chocolate or strawberry? The keyboard will populate three options on the autocomplete menu: "chocolate", "strawberry", and "not sure". You simply click on your decision and it will reply back with the answer. Any time there is a question that asks "item 1 or item 2?" the options will pop up on the keyboard, allowing you to answer without typing.

Volume Control

On the left side of the phone you will find only two buttons – Volume Up and Volume Down. These can be used to change the volume of your ringtones, the volume level of your music and media (during music playback and videos), and your in-call volume (when used during a call).

Right above it you will see the Ring/Silent switch. When switched away from you, silent mode will be activated. Here, your phone will either vibrate or remain silent during notifications, depending on your settings. When switched towards you, it will put the iPhone in ring mode, enabling notifications and calls to emit sound. You can tell which mode it's in just by looking at the switch; a visible red line inside the switch is an indicator that silent mode is turned on.

Multitasking

The iPhone is a powerful computer that is capable of handling multiple programs at once. Introduced in iOS 7, the multitasking feature takes advantage of the phone's raw computing power. To multitask and switch between different apps on the phone, quickly press the home button twice. The screen will become filled with a carousel of screenshots showing you which apps are currently open and running.

Also worth noting is at the top of the multitasking screen you will see recent contacts, and favorite contacts if you have any. Swipe left and right to find the app you want to jump into, and click the app image to confirm the change. The iPhone will immediately pull you out of whichever app you might have been in, and drop you off in the newly opened app.

Continuity

Continuity is not just one feature but actually a suite of features that work together to provide the ultimate seamless experience between all of your Apple devices. Your new iPhone will integrate with your Mac, iPad or iPod in ways that were never possible before. The iPhone 6 and 6 Plus are already equipped with everything you need to take advantage of the continuity features, but Mac computers must have OS X Yosemite or higher, iPods must be at least 5th generation, and iPads must be at least 4th generation.

Before, you were limited to making calls only on your iPhone, but what if it needed charging or you needed to do work on an iPad, iPod, or Mac? Now you can make and receive calls from any of these devices as long as your iPhone is on the same Wi-Fi network, and is signed into the same iCloud and Facetime accounts. The same goes for standard text messages (SMS) and multimedia messages (MMS).

Perhaps the coolest display of integration using continuity is the handoff feature, which basically enables you to pick up any compatible Apple device where you left off on another. For this feature to work, you need to have each device signed into the same iCloud account, and must be within Bluetooth range of each other. This means that if you have Apple devices in your office, you can start filling in your calendar, typing up a Pages document, or browsing the internet using Safari on your Mac for example, and go into the break area and pick up where you left off using your iPhone or iPad without missing a beat. To switch from one device to another, just swipe up from the bottom left of the lock screen or double click the home button and tap the app, then on the other device open up the app.

Handoff can be disabled by doing to Settings > General > Handoff & Suggested Apps.

Control Center

The iPhone 6 comes with a built-in shortcut to some of the most used apps and settings on the phone. To access the Control Center, swipe from the bottom of the phone up to the middle. You will see many different controls: the bottommost row will display the camera, flashlight, timer, and calculator.

The row above it lets you connect to an AirPlay device, and the following row allows you to play or pause music, skip through tracks, and adjust the volume as necessary. Next is the screen brightness slider, and at the very top are 5 frequently used settings that can be toggled on or off: Airplane mode, Wi-Fi, Bluetooth, Do Not Disturb mode, and Screen Rotation.

Chapter 3: Using Pre-Installed Apps

Messaging

More and more smartphone users are staying connected through text messages instead of phone calls, and the iPhone makes it easy to keep in touch with everyone. In addition to sending regular SMS text messages and multimedia messages (pictures, links, video clips and voice notes), you can also use iMessage to interact with other Apple users. This feature allows you to send instant messages to anyone signed into a Mac running OS X Mountain Lion or higher, or any iOS device running iOS 5 or greater.

On the main Messages screen you will be able to see the many different conversations you have going on. You can also delete conversations by swiping from right to left on the conversation you'd like, and tapping the red delete button. New conversations or existing conversations with new messages will be highlighted with a big blue dot next to it, and the Message icon will have a badge displaying the number of unread messages you have, similar to the Mail and Phone icons.

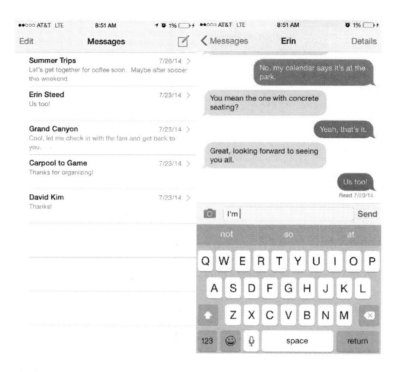

To create a message, click on the Messages icon, then the Compose button in the top right corner.

Once the new message dialog box pops up, click on the plus icon to choose from your contacts list, or just type in the phone number of the person you wish to text. For group messages, just keep adding as many people as you'd like. Finally, click on the bottom field to begin typing your message. To send a photo or video clip, tap on the camera icon towards the bottom left side of the screen.

Camera & Photos

According to Apple, "Every day, people take more photos with the iPhone than with any other camera", and it's for good reason. While the iPhone 6 and 6 Plus retain the same 8 megapixels from previous models, the latest phones are packed with a slew of new features that will make even the savviest photographers excited. You can now film in full HD, which is 1080p at 60 frames per second (fps), in addition to other fun settings like time-lapse panorama and slow motion video capture.

The feature that's been making lots of buzz is called Focus Pixels, which allows the camera lens to rapidly hone in on important objects, in turn enabling much faster, crisper autofocus. On the iPhone 6 Plus, users will enjoy an added bonus – full optical image stabilization, a first for Apple and one of few smartphones to have this capability. What this means for you is that even if the camera is shaky, you will get much sharper images where other cameras would have left you with blurry, unmemorable photographs.

There are two main ways to take a photo with the iPhone. If you need to take a quick snapshot before a moment is lost, the fastest way to the camera is by sliding up the Control Center and tapping on the camera icon. The other way you can access your camera is by tapping on the app icon, just like any other app.

When the camera is open, you will see a few different options you can change. The top part of the screen will contain options for flash mode, auto timer, HDR, and an option to switch between your rear-facing and front-facing cameras. Towards the bottom, you will be able to move the slider left and right to choose between video, photo, square, slow motion, and other options. In the bottom right corner you will find the filter option that allows you to apply filters before you take a picture. The large white button is pressed any time you need to take a photo, and the bottom left icon will open up your photo gallery to view, edit, and delete photos.

Your iPhone is also capable of taking burst shots. As long as it's in either square or photo mode, just press and hold the photo button until you want to stop. The phone will take pictures extremely quick, making it perfect for capturing action shots or sequences.

Due to its improved aperture, the iPhone 6 and 6 Plus can take much better photographs with HDR. High Dynamic Range is best used in high contrast situations, for example if you were taking a picture in broad daylight but under a shady tree, or you were standing on the porch and wanted to take a picture of the street or inside the house. With HDR off, these pictures would look either extremely dark or extremely light. With HDR enabled, the camera will adjust the contrast and shadows to provide a crisp, clear photo.

To view photos, videos and images that you've taken or downloaded, click on Photos on the home screen. You can either scroll up and down, or click on a photo to enlarge it and swipe left and right to navigate between your pictures and videos. You can also share a photo you like by tapping on the Share button at the bottom of the screen.

The share menu will come up and give you several different ways to send your file out, including Messages, Mail, Facebook (if installed), or assign to a contact if you want to put an image to their contact file so it comes up every time they call you.

Calendar

Among the other pre-installed apps that came with your new iPhone, perhaps one of the most used apps you'll encounter is the calendar. You can switch between viewing appointments, tasks, or everything laid out in a one day, one week, or one month view. On the iPhone 6 Plus, turn your phone on its side and you will notice everything switch to landscape mode. A first for the iPhone, many new apps now take advantage of the larger iPhone's 1080p resolution by displaying more information at once, similar to the iPad and iPad mini display. Combine your calendar with email accounts or iCloud to keep your appointments and tasks synced across all of your devices, and never miss another appointment.

Creating an Appointment

To create an appointment, click on the Calendar icon on your home screen. Click on whichever day you would like to set the appointment for, and then tap the plus sign (+) in the corner. Here you will be able to name and edit your event, as well as connect it to an email or iCloud account in order to allow for syncing.

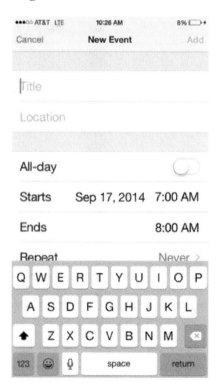

When editing your event, pay special attention to the duration of your event. Select the start and end times, or choose "All Day" if it's an all-day event. You will also have a chance to set it as a recurring event by clicking on Repeat and selecting how often you want it to repeat. In the case of a bill or car payment, for example, you could either select Monthly (on this day) or every 30 days, which are two different things. After you select your repetition, you can also choose how long you'd like for that event to repeat itself: for just one month, a year, forever, and everything in between.

Safari

You may already be familiar with Safari if you've previously owned an iPhone or currently have another Apple product. Safari is Apple's web browser that comes packed with great features.

Browsing and Navigation

Once Safari is launched by tapping on the app's icon, you will be greeted with the home page.

By default the home page displays your favorite websites. At the very top of the page you will see the address bar. Click on it to enter a URL or do a quick web search and tap on the "Go" key to confirm. While you enter text into the address bar you will notice the list of suggestions show up. If you see what you are looking for, click on the words to automatically load that search. At the bottom from left to right is the Back and Forward buttons to navigate between recently viewed web pages, followed by the Share button (also found in other apps like Camera Roll and Messages), Bookmarks, and Tabs.

The Bookmarks section is actually split into three sections: Bookmarks & History, Reading List, and Shared Links. In Bookmarks you will be able to select between viewing your bookmarks and browsing history. To add bookmarks, visit the web page you want to save and press and hold the Bookmark icon, then tap Add Bookmark. Bookmarks can be organized into folders through the same Bookmark icon, just click Edit at the bottom.

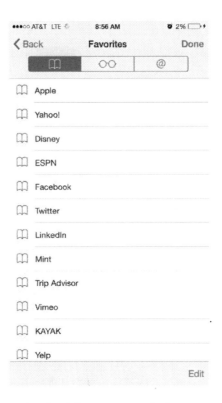

Reading list is the middle icon that looks like a pair of glasses where you can view all of the web pages, blog posts, or articles that you've saved for offline reading. To save a piece of internet literature to your reading list, tap on the Share icon and then click on Add to Reading List. Saved pages can be deleted like a text message by swiping from right to left and tapping on the red Delete button.

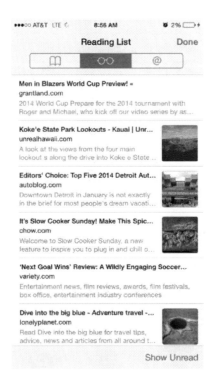

The third tab on the Bookmarks page is where you can view your shared links and subscriptions. Subscriptions can be created from any web page that provides RSS feeds, and your phone will automatically download the latest articles and posts. To subscribe to a site's RSS, visit the website, tap the Bookmark icon, and select Add to Shared Links.

Back on the main Safari home page, the last button found on the bottom right corner is Tabs. Just like the Mac version you can have multiple tabs of web pages open at the same time, and switch between them with ease. To switch the tabs into private mode where your browsing history or cookies will not be saved or recorded, tap the Tabs button and select Private. You will be asked to either close all existing tabs or keep them. If you don't want to lose any tabs that might still be open, opt to keep them. Existing tabs, in addition to any new tabs you open, will now be shielded behind private browsing.

Security

Entering sensitive information on websites is becoming an everyday occurrence now with the ability to shop, bank, and transfer money online. Keychain helps keep all of your usernames, passwords, and credit card information safe, but there are other precautions you can take to ensure you are protected the entire time you are surfing the web.

Phishing (pronounced "fishing") is a dangerous practice that is designed to steal a user's login information and/or credit card details. A phishing website is designed to look exactly like a trusted website (PayPal, Facebook, or your local bank for example). It's easy to not think twice about typing in your Facebook login or PayPal login information since you do it so often, but even though the website may look authentic, you might be inadvertently sending your private information to high tech thieves.

Safari comes built in with an anti-phishing setting to help protect you against sites that are known to be fraudulent or have participated in phishing activities in the past. To turn anti-phishing on, click on Settings > Safari, and toggle on Fradulent Website Warning. Now when you visit a webpage with questionable authenticity, Safari will prompt you with a warning and ask if you'd like to proceed or back out.

If you've ever returned to an online store that still had your shopping cart intact and ready to check out, you've seen cookies in action. Cookies are small bits of data that are stored on websites to provide them with more information about you. It helps websites remember stored data such as saved login information or unfinished shopping carts, but it can also help advertisers target you with specific ads based on your browsing habits. If you'd like to disable cookies, go to Settings > Safari > Block Cookies and select one of the choices. The most common choices are Always Allow, Allow from Websites I Visit (for your frequented web pages), and Always Block. Keep in mind, however, that some sites may need cookies to be enabled in order to work correctly.

Mail

The iPhone lets you add multiple email addresses from virtually any email client you can think of. Yahoo, Gmail, AOL, Exchange, Hotmail, and many more can be added to your phone so that you will be able to check your email no matter where you are. To add an email address, click on the Settings app icon, then scroll to the middle where you'll see Mail, Contacts & Calendar. You will then see logos for the biggest email providers, but if you have another type of email just click on "Other" and continue.

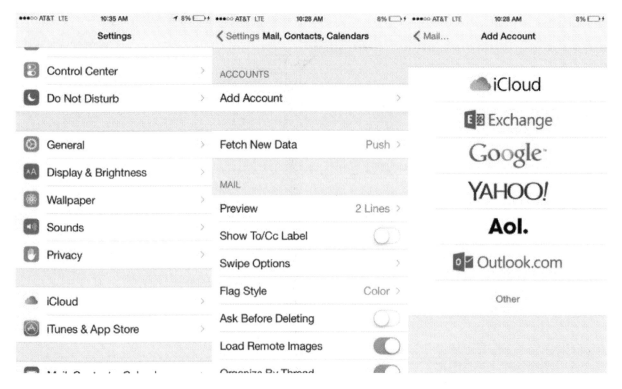

If you don't know your email settings, you will need to visit the Mail Settings Lookup page on the Apple website. There you can type in your entire email address, and the website will show you what information to type and where in order to get your email account working on the phone. The settings change with everyone, so what works for one provider may not work with another. Once you are finished adding as many email accounts as you may need, you will be able to click on the Mail app icon on your phone's home screen, and view each inbox separately, or all at once.

Maps

The Maps app is back and better than ever. After Apple parted ways with Google Maps several years ago, Apple decided to develop its own, made-for-iPhone map and navigation system. The result is a beautiful travel guide that takes full advantage of the newest iPhone resolutions. Full screen mode allows every corner of the phone to be filled with the app, and there's an automatic night mode just like with iBooks. You'll be able to search for places, restaurants, gas stations, concert halls, and other venues near you at any time, and turn-by-turn navigation is available for walking, biking, driving, or commuting. Traffic is updated in real time, so if an accident occurs ahead of you or there is construction going on, Maps will offer a faster alternative and warn you of the potential traffic jam.

The turn-by-turn navigation is easy to understand without being distracting, and the 3D view makes potentially difficult scenarios (like highway exits that come up abruptly) much more pleasant.

To set up navigation, tap on the Maps icon. At the top left corner there will be what looks like a curved arrow icon. Click on it and enter your destination once prompted. When you find your destination's address, click on Route, and choose between walking or driving directions. For hands-free navigation, press and hold the home button to enable Siri (which will be discussed in the next section) and say "Navigate to" or "Take me to" followed by the address or name of the location that you'd like to go to.

Siri

Apple's digital personal assistant Siri has grown in uses and popularity since its debut on the iPhone 4S. The possibilities are endless when it comes to what you can do with Siri, as long as there is a solid data connection either through 3G, 4G LTE, or Wi-Fi. Here are just a few things you can say to Siri:

- "Navigate me to [place]" or "Take me to [place]" will start your GPS and point you in the right direction

- "Text [contact name] [message]" to send someone a text message

- "Call [contact]" to dial a phone number from your contacts list

- "Wake me up at [time]" will set the phone's alarm

- "I have a doctor's appointment at [time]" to add an appointment to your calendar.

- You can even create relationships that Siri can recognize. For example, say "Tina is my mom" or "Mark is my boyfriend" to establish a relationship, and from then on you can simply say "call my mom" or "my boyfriend is picking me up at noon tomorrow" and Siri will make the connection for you.

To enable Siri, go to Settings > General > Siri and toggle it on. After Siri is enabled, you can engage her by pressing and holding the home button until you hear the signature "ding" sound that shows Siri is ready to listen.

Your new iPhone (and any other device running iOS 8 or higher) will also have a new feature called "Hey Siri", which you can also toggle in this same screen. The Hey Siri feature works as long as your phone has iOS 8, is plugged into a charger, and you have the setting enabled through the settings menu.

This allows you to call Siri by simply saying "Hey Siri" followed by your command, removing the need to press and hold the home button. It's a great way to stay safe and hands-free while driving, and convenient if you are reading at night and have the phone charging on the nightstand, but need to send a quick message or check one last thing before sleep.

Health

The release of the latest iPhone models brought with it a much greater focus on one's health, and as such, the new iPhones come with the Health app. The Health app keeps track of many different things pertaining to your health, including calories burned, your weight, heart rate, body measurements, and even an emergency card that lets you store important health information such as your blood type and allergies in the event of an emergency. There are four different tabs at the bottom of the app:

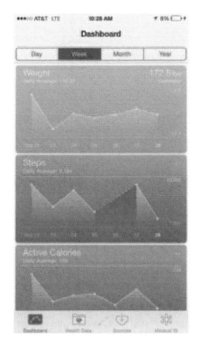

Dashboard

Here you will be able to see an at-a-glance view of your vitals, including calories burned, weight, and heart rate. You will be able to choose between one day's worth of information, a week, month, and even a year if you'd like to see how your health today compares to last year.

Health Data

This page is the main hub where you can find and store all of your information. It's broken down into a few general categories like body measurements, fitness, nutrition, sleep, and vitals, but can include even the smallest details like your blood sugar level, glucose levels, sleep patterns, current medications, and more.

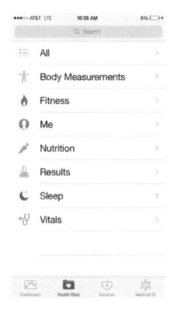

Sources

Sources weren't available at launch, but it's finally been released to much acclaim. This section is where you can control who or what can access your health information, as well as who can send you information regarding your health.

It's meant to connect to third party apps or doctors in order to send them accurate information about you, and a quick snapshot of how your days are even when you aren't visiting the doctor. This could be especially beneficial to you if you have a health condition that requires more frequent monitoring, such as diabetes.

Medical ID

Here is the virtual emergency card we mentioned earlier. This is the place to store all the important information about you in case a medical worker needs it in the event of an emergency. Enter in your blood type, allergies (medical or otherwise), chronic health conditions, diseases, medications, emergency contact, and anything else you can think of so whoever is treating you can access revenant information without wasting time.

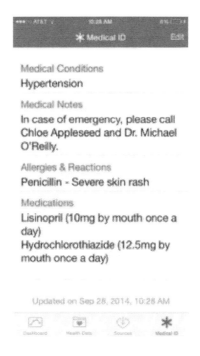

iBooks

Now that the iPhone 6 and 6 Plus feature bigger screens, you can probably do more and more reading on your phone while reading less on your iPad. If that's the case, you will love the new version of iBooks. Your favorite books can be read in complete full screen mode, and flick through the pages to enjoy that classic page-turning animation. Trying to organize your library and keep track of which books you have left to complete a book series? Now iBooks automatically sorts books by series, keeping everything neat and tidy for you.

The latest updates enable you to upload quotes directly to your favorite social networking or blogging site, and if you see a word you aren't familiar with, just press and hold it until the word in question becomes highlighted, then select Dictionary. Additionally, night time reading has gotten easier with the night theme. Dim or shut the lights off while reading and iBooks will automatically switch to night mode for easier viewing. Turn the lights back on, and the theme will switch back to normal reading mode.

App Store

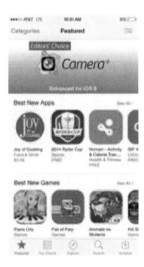

The App Store - the iPhone's meat and potatoes. Here you will be able to add as much functionality as you can possibly think of to your phone. Need a maritime GPS, restaurant manager, CRM tracker, or an accounting app? These and many, many more can be found in the App Store, where over 1.3 million apps are waiting to be explored with more added each and every day.

You can sort through the options by category (including business, finance, education, reference, games, and productivity), top free, top paid, and editor's picks. Of course, if you'd prefer to just search for whatever comes to mind, you can also select the search icon on the bottom tray or the magnifying glass in the upper right corner to search for particular titles.

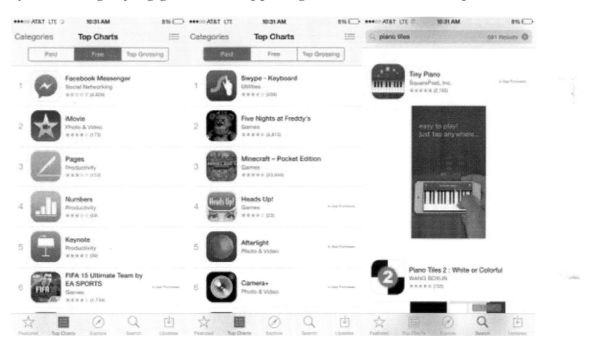

At the end of this guide, we provide you with a comprehensive list of the top 25 free apps, as well as the top 25 paid apps to get you started.

iTunes

The iTunes app found on your home screen opens the biggest digital music store in the world. You will be able to purchase and download not just music, but also countless movies, TV shows, audiobooks, and more. On the iTunes home page you can also find a What's Hot section, collections of music, and new releases.

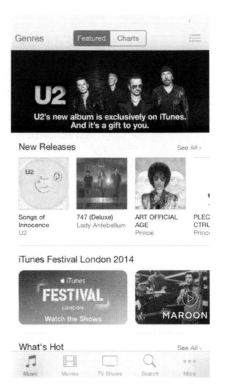

At the top you will see the option to view either featured media, or browse through the top charts. On the upper left corner is the Genres button. Clicking Genres will bring up many different types of music to help refine your search.

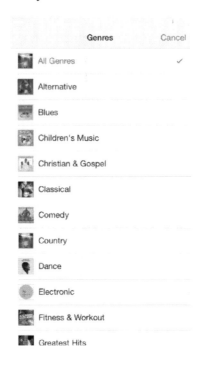

When you find a song, album, or movie that you want to download, you will be greeted with a screen displaying information such as ratings, reviews, related, a track list, short description, and the price.

If you already have iTunes on your Mac or PC, you can sync your iPhone with it by connecting through Wi-Fi or a USB cable. If you have iTunes automatically sync with devices any time you plug them in, no further steps are necessary. If not, you can connect wirelessly by having both devices on the same Wi-Fi network. On the computer, go to iTunes, find your phone's name, select Summary, and then Sync with this iPhone over Wi-Fi. For this feature to work though, your iPhone needs to be plugged into a power source until the sync is complete.

To physically connect the two devices, plug your phone into the computer using the USB sync cable that came with the iPhone, and wait for your phone's name to come up on the computer screen. Once it does you will be able to choose between a few different options including automatically sync every time the iPhone is connected to iTunes, or choose just a few categories to sync like music or photos. Contacts and calendars used to be synced through iTunes, but today they are typically backed up through iCloud instead. Syncing contacts even when they are stored on iCloud could result in doubles of every contact you have stored.

Weather

You can use your iPhone's location services and GPS to help you navigate to your destinations, but other apps can use it to display localized information. The Weather app is one such example of this. Opening it up will immediately show you basic weather information based on your current location. To get more detailed information, you can swipe left and right on the middle section to scroll through the hourly forecast, and swipe up and down on the bottom section to scroll through the 10 day forecast.

You can add more cities by clicking on the list icon towards the bottom right and searching for the city name. Once you've added cities, you can scroll between cities to see real-time weather information for each location by swiping left or right, and the number of cities you have added are shown at the bottom in the form of small dots.

Notes

The Notes app allows you to create, edit and store notes and quick memos. The app can be used to set aside an important snippet of information, a grocery list, a list of hotels to research, or anything else you might need to notate.

Notes can be stored and backed up through iCloud, and they can also be synced with other accounts like Yahoo or Gmail. To sync notes with an account, go to Settings > Mail, Contacts, Calendars and toggle Notes on. To filter notes by account, go back to the Notes app, click on Accounts, and select the account you want to focus on. You can also set which account will be the default for future accounts by going to Settings > Notes and selecting the account.

Apple Pay & NFC

Near Field Communication, or NFC, has been around for several years now. The biggest concern surrounding NFC, and perhaps the reason why it hasn't caught on, was how relatively easy it can be to steal someone's information from a smartphone or connected device. With the release of the iPhone 6 and 6 Plus, Apple announced their own take on NFC technology and NFC-enabled payments with Apple Pay. Both the iPhone 6 and 6 Plus are the only iPhones able to work with Apple Pay, and the company is expected to roll the systems out around October. Scores of partners including Visa, Mastercard, American Express, Bank of America, Macy's, Dunkin' Donuts, McDonald's, and many other companies small and large are already on board, installing terminals that will work with Apple Pay.

In response to lingering concerns over security, Apple describes Apple Pay as the most secure way to purchase goods and services, a viable replacement for the ancient, unsafe technology found within credit cards. Using a special Secure Element SIM card, the iPhone does not store or use credit card numbers at all, and instead generates a unique serial number each time a purchase is made, which then expires shortly afterward. With the use of Touch ID, purchases can be made in just a few steps instead of the long process currently used by everyone, and should a phone get lost, credit card information is still safe since it isn't stored on the phone, and payments can be disabled through Find My iPhone.

Chapter 4: Customizing Phone and Features

Arranging Apps and Screens

Over time, you will download and use many different apps, and organizing these can prove to be a real challenge. Luckily, the iPhone has a few different ways you can move your apps around to keep everything neat and tidy, while leaving the most important or frequently used apps only a click away.

By default, the apps just appear in a grid on your home screen in the order they are downloaded. Download more apps than the home screen can hold and another home screen will automatically be created to accommodate more icons.

You can organize apps and move them around by pressing and holding on an icon. You will notice the icons will start to shake, and at this point you can continue holding down the app and moving it around. To bring it to another screen, drag it to the very edge of the screen for a moment until it changes to another screen. You can also group several related apps together into folders by dragging one app icon into another.

Wallpaper & Brightness

You can customize your phone's home screen and lock screen wallpaper, as well as the brightness, by going to Settings > Display & Brightness or Settings > Wallpaper. You will be able to choose between static and dynamic images to use as your wallpaper (dynamic images tend to drain a little more battery than normal), and set that image as either your home screen, lock screen, or both. The brightness slider can also be moved around to change the brightness to something a little more comfortable and easier to see for you.

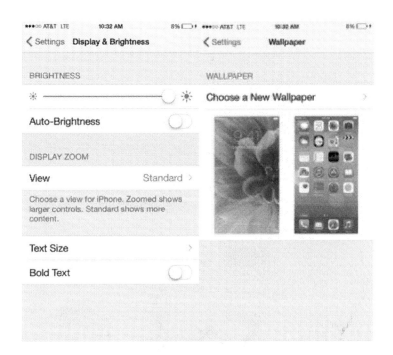

If you find yourself constantly having to change it, however, it might be best to just toggle the Auto-Brightness on. This can also help preserve battery since it will change brightness depending on how bright it is outside, so if you are indoors for a long period of time it will keep the screen dimmer than you might normally have it.

Ringtones & Sound

To access your ringtones and volume settings, go to Settings > Sounds. There are options letting you change everything from a mail or text message notification sound to your phone's ringtone and vibration settings.

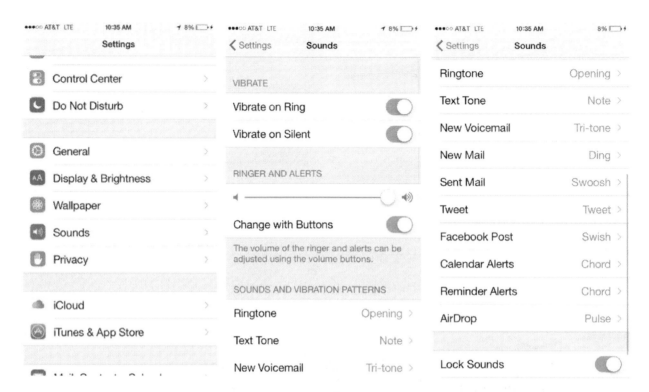

You will also be able to toggle between keyboard clicks on or off, if you don't like hearing each button pressed when you are typing a message. Since the iPhone is so popular, one cool feature is the ability to create your own vibration patterns by clicking on Vibration > Create New Vibration and then tapping whatever pattern you would like. Changing it from the standard vibration will help your phone's notifications stand out if it's among several other iPhones on a table.

Accessibility

The iPhone is designed to be enjoyed by everyone, and comes with several different features to allow users with disabilities to use the phone easier.

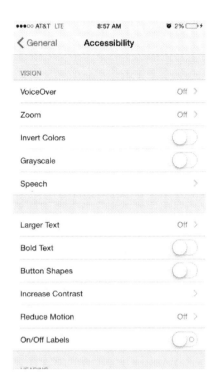

Zoom

The Zoom feature itself is not new, but iOS 8 tweaks Zoom and provides more robust tools for controlling it where and when you want it. Now you'll be able to zoom the keyboard, have the zoom follow wherever you are focused, and blow up a portion of the screen between 1000-1500 percent while keeping the rest of the screen in its native size.

Text

If you have a tough time viewing the on-screen text or just want to avoid unnecessary eye fatigue, you can enlarge the font by going to Settings > Accessibility > Larger Type and toggling on Larger Dynamic Type. At the bottom, you will also be able to drag a slider indicating how large you'd like the font on the phone to be. Maybe the font is large enough, but you need it to be heavier in order to increase legibility. If that's the case, go to Settings > General > Accessibility and toggle Bold Text. You will need to reboot your iPhone for the changes to take complete effect.

If you prefer the phone to have darker colors overall, you can invert the colors by going to Settings > General > Accessibility and toggling Invert Colors on or off.

VoiceOver

Those with significant visual impairment will benefit from using VoiceOver, a built-in system that will speak out every single action and menu item that you touch, including scrolling and clicking links. It can be activated by rapidly clicking the home button three times, or going to Settings > General > Accessibility > VoiceOver and toggling between on and off. Also in this menu you will find options for speaking rate, hints, sound effects, and pitch change to shake off that robotic voice you may remember.

Chapter 5: Maintenance and Security

Closing Apps

As mentioned earlier, your iPhone has the ability to handle multiple apps and tasks at once, and most of those apps can run in the background. If you leave too many apps open or a data-hogging app is left running in the background and forgotten about, however, you could greatly reduce battery life and also increase data usage without even realizing it. To close any unwanted apps you no longer need open, simply click on the home button twice to open up the multitasking menu, and swipe through the open programs to find the one you want to close. Instead of clicking on the image to switch to the desired app once you locate it, just swipe the app's image up and it will disappear, signaling that it closed down. Repeat as necessary until you've closed out all unneeded apps.

Extending Battery Life

Both the iPhone 6 and 6 Plus come with much larger batteries than their predecessors:

	iPhone 5S	iPhone 6	iPhone 6 Plus
Talk Time	Up to 10 hours on 3G	Up to 14 hours on 3G	Up to 24 hours on 3G
Standby Time	Up to 8 days (384 hours)	Up to 10 days (250 hours)	Up to 16 days (250 hours)
Internet Use	Up to 8 hours on LTE	Up to 10 hours on LTE	Up to 12 hours on LTE
Video Playback	Up to 10 hours	Up to 11 hours	Up to 14 hours
Audio Playback	Up to 40 hours	Up to 50 hours	Up to 80 hours

To really get a good handle on your battery life, turn on battery percentage by going to

Settings > General > Usage > Battery Usage and toggling Battery Percentage on. In this menu you will also find the time since last full charge, separated into Usage and Standby. Usage only includes the time spent actually using the phone, whether it's for making a call, surfing the web, or sending an email, and excludes time spent locked and in your pocket or purse. Standby, on the other hand, includes all time elapsed since the iPhone was taken off the charger. Even though the batteries on the new phones faced tremendous improvements, there are still a few tips you can use to make the battery last even longer.

iOS 8 comes with a new feature that lets you keep track of how much battery each app is using whether its running in the foreground or background. This is a great way to tell if there is one app in particular that is responsible for draining your battery faster than usual. To access the Battery Usage menu, click on Settings > General > Usage > Battery Usage. What you are looking for here is an app that you aren't using, but it's still using a significant portion of your battery. Any app that is using up the battery while inactive means there are probably taxing background processes going on. You can either uninstall that app, or if you would like to keep it, just disable the background app refresh by going to Settings > General > Background App Refresh and toggling it off. Some iPhone users choose to just shut background refresh on all apps and manually refresh when they open an app. This will greatly improve the already powerful battery life, but it will come at the expense of having important apps automatically update such as the weather or navigation.

Another great feature included in iOS 8 is a new setting for location services, which allow the phone to track your location for use in apps such as GPS, Siri, and many more. Now you are able to turn location services on only when you need them instead of all the time. This will end up saving you battery because the GPS is not constantly searching for signal at all times. To change this setting, go to Settings > Privacy > Location Services and select While Using the App.

Lastly, another way to get more juice out of your battery is by increasing the time between email refreshes. There are two ways your email could be set up: Push or Fetch. You can find out how your email accounts are currently set up by going to Settings > Mail, Contacts and Calendars > Fetch New Data. Push means that each time you receive an email the phone will immediately display it for you and sound a notification, but Fetch searches for mail only by specific intervals. If you don't mind receive emails periodically instead of immediately as they come in, setting the Fetch interval to every 30 minutes or even an hour can greatly increase your battery life.

Security

Passcode (dos and don'ts, tips, etc.)

In this day and age, it's important to keep your device secure. You may or may not want to set up a touch ID (you will read more about it next), but at the very least it's a good idea to maintain a passcode. Anytime your phone is unlocked, restarted, updated, or erased, it will require a passcode before allowing entry into the phone. To set up a passcode for your iPhone, go to Settings > Passcode, and click on Turn Passcode On. You will be prompted to enter a 4 digit passcode, then re-enter to confirm. Here are a few tips to follow for maximum security:

Do's

DO create a unique passcode that only you would know

DO change it every now and then to keep it unknown

DO select a passcode that can be easily modified later when it's time to change passcodes

Don'ts

DON'T use a simple passcode like 1234 or 5678

DON'T use your birthday or birth year

DON'T use a passcode someone else might have (for example, a shared debit card pin)

DON'T go right down the middle (2580) or sides (1470 or 3690)

Touch ID

Your iPhone 6 comes with a fingerprint scanner called Touch ID that allows you to unlock your phone, activate Apple Pay, make purchases in the App Store, iTunes, or iBooks, and verify yourself with just the tap of a button. To set up a fingerprint or two (you're allowed to store several), go to Settings > Passcode > Touch ID and enable it. Then select Add a Fingerprint. You will be brought to a screen prompting you to place your finger (don't click!) on the home button. It's important to hold the phone as you normally would, otherwise you run the risk of storing incorrect or distorted fingerprints.

Once the phone is comfortable in your hand, place the finger that you'd like to store on the home button, careful once again not to click it. You will see the gray fingerprint image on the screen start to fill up with pink. Remove your finger, and gently place it down again, with small variations on your placement.

Repeat this process until the entire fingerprint image is filled in, and you will automatically be taken to the next screen titled "Adjust your Grip". Here, you will need to add even more variations of your fingerprint in order to capture the edges of your fingerprint. Follow the same steps as the previous screen, and soon you will complete the fingerprint scanning process. To activate it, lock the screen and enter your passcode, then lock it again. After it's locked, you can unlock it with one finger by clicking the home button to turn the screen on, then gently resting your finger on the button. The fingerprint should register and the phone will unlock. The only times a passcode will still be required is when you initially set up a passcode, when you restart the phone, when you enter the Passcode settings, and when more than 48 hours have elapsed since you've unlocked the phone.

iCloud

To really get the full effect of Apple's carefully created ecosystem and be a part of it, you will need to create an iCloud account. Simply put, iCloud is a powerful cloud system that will seamlessly coordinate all of your important devices. The cloud can be a little difficult to understand, but the best way to think about it is like a storage unit that lives in a secure part of the internet. You are allocated a certain amount of space, and you can put the things that mean the most to you here to keep safe. In the case of iCloud, Apple gives you 5 GB for free.

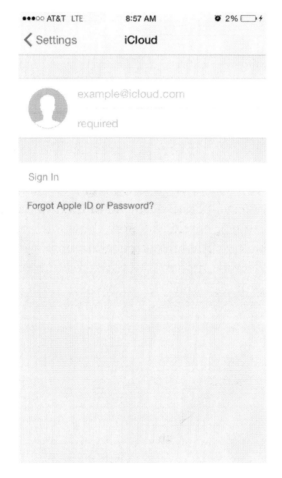

Your phone lets you automatically back up certain files such as your photos, mail, contacts, calendars, reminders, and notes. In the event that your phone is damaged beyond repair or is lost or stolen, your data will still be stored safely on iCloud. To retrieve your information, you can either log onto icloud.com on a Mac or PC, or log into your iCloud account on another iPhone to load the information onto that phone.

With the introduction of iOS 8 and the iPhone 6 and 6 Plus, Apple rolled out a few major changes. You will now be able to store even more types of documents using iCloud Drive and access them from any smartphone, tablet, or computer. Additionally, up to 6 family members will now be able to share purchases from iTunes, iBooks, and the App Store, removing the need to buy an app twice simply because you and a loved one have two different iCloud accounts.

For users who will need more than 5 GB, Apple has dramatically reduced the cost of iCloud:

• 20 GB is $0.99 per month

• 200 GB is $3.99 per month

• 500 GB is $9.99 per month

• 1 TB (1024 GB) is $19.99 per month

Encryption

With all of the personal and sensitive information that can be stored on iCloud, security is understandably a very real concern. Apple agrees with this, and protects your data with high level 128-bit AES encryption. Keychain, which you will learn about next, uses 256-bit AES encryption - the same level of encryption used by all of the top banks who need high levels of security for their data. According to Apple, the only things not protected with encryption through iCloud is mail (because email clients already provide their own security) and iTunes in the Cloud, since music does not contain any personal information.

Keychain

Have you logged onto a website for the first time in ages and forgot what kind of password you used? This happens to everyone; some websites require special characters or phrases, while others require small 8 character passwords. iCloud comes with a highly encrypted feature called Keychain that allows you to store passwords and login information in one place. Any of your Apple devices synced with the same iCloud account will be able to load the data from Keychain without any additional steps.

To activate and start using Keychain, simply click on Settings > iCloud and toggle Keychain on, then follow the prompts. After you've added accounts and passwords to Keychain, your Safari browser will automatically fill in fields while you remain logged into iCloud. If you are ready to checkout after doing some online shopping, for example, the credit card information will automatically pre-fill so you don't have to enter any sensitive information at all.

Appendix A: Best 20 Paid Apps

Minecraft ($6.99)

One of the most popular indie video games, Minecraft was developed for PC originally, but its overwhelming popularity prompted the video game's creators to release it on major video game consoles, Android phones, and of course, iOS devices. The Minecraft craze is showing no signs of slowing down – stuffed animals, shirts, and real world building kits resembling Lego blocks are being sold everywhere. The biggest draw to this game is the ability to create virtually anything you'd like, whether it's a small, simple town or a full scale replica of your home or favorite Irish castle. While the game has been out on iOS for 4 years now, the game continues to receive updates periodically. In Minecraft, you can create entire worlds as you imagine them, and play in worlds designed by other users. You can also gather resources to build and defend your construction sites, craft items, and battle enemies. There are several different modes of play including Survival which forces the player to continue to gather food and resources in order to battle hunger and avoid losing.

Swype ($0.99)

One of the most popular third-party Android keyboards has finally made its way onto iOS 8 devices. Developed by Nuance Communications, Swype's claim to fame is its ability to let you slide your finger across letters to form words and sentences. Small features like automatically adding a space after each swipe and learning unique words as you type make this a must-have for new iPhone owners who want to enjoy quick one handed typing on their larger screens. The iPhone version comes with five great looking themes, while the iPad features two themes. In order for Swype to work correctly, you must have Guided Access either shut off, or enabled with "Full Access". To do this, visit the menu by going to Settings > General > Accessibility > Guided Access and make your selection there.

Afterlight ($0.99)

When you take a snapshot with the iPhone 6 and its new camera, you might capture the perfect shot but wish that the coloring was a little different. Or perhaps you are happy with the color but would like to add a texture to the image or crap a certain part out. All of this and more can be done with Afterlight, a simple but powerful tool that will help you bring a photo to life. The feature highlights include more than 50 filters and textures, cropping, transforming, adjustments, and frames. While editing a photo, you can see the changes in real time as you move the sliders, and when you are happy with the finished product, you can export the image in a number of formats and resolutions, then post directly to major channels like Messages, Instagram, Facebook, or just the Camera Roll.

Documents to Go ($16.99)

Documents to Go is the #1 selling mobile Microsoft Office suite, and allows you to create and edit Word, Excel, and Powerpoint documents, in addition to viewing Adobe PDF files. Designed for productivity on the go, this app provides seamless integration with other devices on Wi-Fi, as well the best cloud services including iCloud, Dropbox, Google Drive, and SugarSync. Another feature that makes this a top choice among many is its ability to view PowerPoint files in full presentation mode.

Clear ($4.99)

Clear is to tasks and to-do lists as Mailbox is to email – it's designed to help you be more productive, keep up with all of the tasks you have to get done, and stop procrastination in its tracks. Lists of tasks and chores are created and separated as you see fit, and the iCloud integration will provide seamless transitions between your Apple devices. Pick a list to focus on, and use several different gestures to mark them complete, save them for later using reminders, or delete old items. Each list can be customized with themes and color to help distinguish between them, and lists can be labeled so you know for sure which list is currently being used and edited. With the new iOS 8 update, you'll also be able to view tasks for the day in your iPhone's notification panel under Today.

PCalc ($9.99)

PCalc is an extremely powerful, all-purpose scientific calculator that can be used by everyone including students, engineers, scientists, developers, and architects. Buying this app removes the need for buying expensive physical calculators, as the features are almost endless. Unit conversions, undo, redo, scientific notation, binary and hexademical conversions, and engineering notation are just some of the things PCalc can do. You can customize the look and feel of the calculator to better match your needs and preferences, and buttons can also be created and added to the calculator. These buttons can streamline certain tasks you need to keep repeating, such as converting units or storing constants. The iOS 8 update features a mini calculator you can use in the widget area to perform quick calculations on your iPhone 6 whenever necessary.

Sky Guide ($1.99)

If you've had an iPhone or iOS product in the past, you may remember this app as being one of the first (and best) apps for viewing and identifying the stars during the night. It's come a long way since then. The app remains one of the best ways to view stars and learn more about them, and now works during the day time as well. In addition to finding out about stars, planets, and entire galaxies, the app now shows you charted paths for satellites so you can plan ahead and watch a satellite pass overhead. The larger screens on the new iPhones will do justice to the amazing visuals presented by this app, and the minimalist design will really let you focus on what matters during app use – the stars above.

1Password ($9.99)

It seems like today we have more passwords than we can even remember. Each site requires different passwords with different rules (some with symbols or some with capital letters, for example) and it's becoming harder and harder to remember them all. Luckily, 1Password provides a highly secure, complete solution whether you just need to store passwords for your favorite online stores, or need to store sensitive information along with passwords and other documents. The app makes use of a single Master Password that allows entry into its database, and the latest update enables the use of Touch ID on the iPhone. 1Password can store and save information so you can pre-fill out online forms or purchase orders, and shop or exchange sensitive data safely. You can also create incredibly long and complex passwords with the password generator, and let 1Password do the remembering for you.

Support for Dropbox and iCloud integration comes standard, so you can sync and access your information from a wide variety of devices. Lastly, another unique feature that sets 1Password apart is the ability to create "vaults", or areas where passwords and login information can be stored and shared with different people, such as a work vault for co-workers to share common info, or a family vault to share information with your closest loved ones.

SAS Survival Guide ($5.99)

Based on the best-selling book by John "Lofty" Wiseman, the SAS Survival Guide is a complete reproduction of the original 400 page book, but optimized for reading on an iPhone. It's designed to teach you world-class survival skills in a variety of potentially hostile environments including desert, urban, and sea coast, with a large quiz that includes over 100 questions at the end. The survival guide also covers important topics like hunting, first aid, setting up shelter, finding food, and identifying wild food. It even includes a Morse code converter that allows you to type a message, and the entire phone will become a white screen that sends out Morse code corresponding with what you wrote.

The app is designed to run without the need for an internet connection, though instructional videos will require a connection in order to stream. An extra in-app purchase for $3.99 is available in the form of an urban survival guide. The urban edition covers topics that can occur a little closer to home if you live in the city, such as terrorism, DIY power tools, welding, and machinery, and handling dangerous fires and chemicals.

ProCamera 8 ($3.99)

Released just weeks after the iPhone 6 and 6 Plus, ProCamera 8 is a follow up to the smash hit ProCamera 7 and is optimized for use with iOS 8 devices. To get the full power of ProCamera 8, an additional in-app purchase will need to be made for vividHDR ($1.99). The partnership of these two apps pays off however, with the best HDR camera the iPhone has ever had. With the new iPhone's improved camera and faster autofocus, the HDR feature is now lightning fast and beautiful. Full manual controls let you change ISO, aperture, shutter speed, white balance, contrast, and so much more. The app itself is designed to be quick, responsible, and everything is laid out in such a way as to minimize distractions while trying to get that perfect shot.

Sketchbook Mobile ($1.99)

Brought to you by Autodesk, the makers of powerful and very well-known software including AutoCAD, 3D Studio Max and Maya, is Sketchbook Mobile, an app designed to let you create professional-grade drawings, paintings, and sketches on a mobile platform. The larger iPhone screens will make you feel at home while you explore and use the many different pencils, brushes, and edges provided by the app. The controls feel fluid and uncluttered, and the use of Steady Stroke will make sure your drawings come out looking clean. You can change everything from the canvas size and layout, to the number of layers you'd like to work with. Works in progress or the finished products can be saved to iCloud or Dropbox,

Spotify ($9.99 per month)

Even though Spotify has recently released a free version, it's covered in commercials and doesn't let you choose the music you want to play, leaving you stuck in shuffle mode. The popular music player app allows premium members to find and listen to any artist or song they want at any time without any limits. Songs, albums, and even entire discographies can be saved to a phone, tablet, or computer for offline use to reduce data consumption, and playlists can be made of your favorite tunes. If you are in the mood for music but can't think of a particular artist you'd like to listen to, or if you need ambient music, you can search for collections of related songs built around a specific theme. For example, some of the collections are made specifically for high intensity cardio, studying, first date, and lifting heavy weights. There are even collections made to showcase theme music from some of the most popular films. If you're a current student, enjoy a 50 percent off promotion by Spotify that will cut the monthly cost from $9.99 to just $4.99 per month. All you need is a valid school email address to qualify.

Pandora ($3.99 per month)

Pandora is a powerful online radio that has seen numerous changes over the years. Much like Spotify, there is a free version that comes with commercials, and you're only allowed to skip songs a certain number of times. Where it differs from Spotify is how music lovers should use this. It's not meant as a music library where you can find favorite songs and artists to listen to, but instead it's supposed to be a music discovery tool. You create stations based on an artist or song, and music similar to that song or artist will begin playing for you. Once a song appears, you can either give the song a thumbs up or a thumbs down to let the app's algorithm know if it should continue finding songs similar to the current one, or avoid similar ones. It's a great way to find new music you might like, and the personalized stations provide much better music than a regular radio station when you want to just hit "Play" and not fuss with it too much.

Sleep Cycle Alarm ($0.99)

This is not just another alarm clock app for the iPhone. Sleep Cycle Alarm is a special app that not only wakes you up when you need to, but does so by tracking your sleep cycles and waiting for the optimal time to wake you. As we sleep, we go through different phases and cycles that range from very deep sleep to light sleep. When we wake up suddenly during the deeper phases of sleep, we awake feeling confused, irritable, dazed, or foggy. Waking up during the lighter periods gets us feeling energized, alert, and wide awake.

The app uses the iPhone's highly sensitive, built-in accelerometer to track your movements during sleep, and creates a 30 minute window to wake you up at the best time during a light sleeping phase. For example, if you set the alarm to wake you up at 6am but your light sleep cycle peaks around 5:30 or 5:45am, the alarm will instead go off at that time. You can view and track your sleep quality over a span of time, and see the patterns of sleep throughout the night. After using this app for a week, you will be able to see exactly how well you slept each night, and from there decide if you should modify your bedtime a little differently to improve sleep quality. According to the developers, the best and safest place to store your iPhone during sleep is directly beneath your head, under the pillow.

7 Minute Workout ($1.99)

This app is perfect for those with a busy lifestyle but a desire to get or stay in shape. The simple, light design was developed to be easy to use and set up. There are 12 exercises in total, and no weights or gym memberships are necessary since they all use only your bodyweight. There are varying degrees of intensity depending on your physical ability and skill, and each exercise lasts only 30 seconds with a period of rest for 10 seconds in between exercises. The entire routine really does only take 7 minutes, and because it uses just bodyweight, you can work out in the privacy of your hotel room or bedroom whenever you have the time. Everything is spoken with voice, so you can just start the app, place the phone on a dresser, table, or on the floor next to you, and proceed with the workout. If an exercise is new to you, don't worry – the app outlines and explains each of the exercises so you can be sure to perform it properly and safely. With the latest iOS 8 update, integration with the iPhone's Health app comes built in, allowing you to sync this program up with all of your other health devices and apps.

Wolfram Alpha ($2.99)

Wolfram Alpha is truly a technological marvel. The app is a hub of information where you can ask questions or complete searches, and a supercomputer will quickly analyze information, crunch numbers, and send back a response in record time without draining much data or battery life. The developer boasts the app is suitable for anyone needing information, no matter how complex –3 engineers, parents, economists, analysts, nutritionists, pilots, physicians, journalists, and everything in between. Doing searches on Wolfram Alpha requires a different mindset than just doing a simple Google or Wikipedia search. Each query will return a definitive, factual answer that's been verified by experts. Doing two searches, one for "speed" and the other for "absorption coefficient of sound moist air at 30C and 20 percent and 6000ft" both produced clear, authoritative answers. It's this flexibility and computational ability that makes Wolfram Alpha a powerful tool to have in the palm of your hands.

Ultimate Guitar Tabs ($2.99)

If you're a guitar player and use tabs or chord charts to learn music, you've no doubt come across the Ultimate Guitar website, an online repository of countless tabs, chords, lessons, and equipment reviews. The Ultimate Guitar Tabs app lets you download, open, view and play tabs on your iPhone. Features include custom speed and tempo adjustments, auto scroll, easy to read chord diagrams, built in tuner, and a metronome to help improve your technique. On top of being able to download and play back tabs, you can also create and edit your own tabs with the program, and compose entire arrangements using an assortment of instruments like drums, bass, and even entire string sections. Certainly a must-have for every guitarist.

JEFIT Pro Workout ($4.99)

This is the ultimate app for anyone looking to get serious results at the gym. The key to a successful weight lifting routine is variety and tracking as much data as possible. JEFIT Pro enables you to do all that and more. The app comes with more than 1300 different exercises, each complete with their own full description and animation to show you how to perform it, and the ability to create your own workout routines or download from the hundreds of user-created routines available online through its website. You will be able to keep a log of how much weight you lift, track body measurements, and join the community of other JEFIT users.

Yoga Studio ($3.99)

If you are finding yourself unable to make it to yoga classes due to a busy schedule or classes that just don't work with your schedule, then bring the classes to you with Yoga Studio. This simple app provides a total of 65 yoga and meditation classes spanning beginner, intermediate, and advanced difficulties. These difficulties are further customized by choosing length (15, 30, or 60 minute sessions), and selecting a specialty such as strength, balance, flexibility, meditation, or a mix. The classes are all filmed in high quality, full HD video so it will feel like you're right there, especially with the iPhone's improved screen resolution. There are more than 280 poses spread out across the classes, and each one is filmed separately so you can actually combine poses in whichever order you prefer, and save that video as a whole new class. Additionally, you can schedule any class whether pre-made or custom and sync it with your calendar to build a routine for yourself.

CamCard ($0.99)

Do you come home from parties or networking events with loads of business cards in each pocket and find yourself just tossing them into a drawer, filing cabinet, or the garbage? It might be time to find a better solution. CamCard is a simple app with one purpose: store and organize your business cards. Using the iPhone's camera, you scan in the front and back of a business card, and CamCard will automatically convert it into a digital format for you. You can then add that person to your contacts list, and each field will be filled out correctly. Users of the app will also be able to send and receive the digital business cards either through QR code scanning or Nearby Contacts. Cards can also be exported by text, email, or QR code, allowing you to send your information or the information of an important contact to others.

JotNot Pro ($2.99)

While it's main claim to fame is the ability to replace a fax machine, JotNot Pro works great as a replacement scanner as well. You can scan documents, business cards, photographs, posters, and anything else you can take a picture of and JotNot will let you store and share it. Documents can be scanned in easily with just a few clicks, and if the image was taken at an angle, you can move and edit the borders to change the perspective with no noticeable distortion. If you need to email documents but have a file size limit, the app will let you change resolution and file size until it meets your criteria. Exporting options include Dropbox, Adobe PDF, Evernote, Google Docs, and email. You can even fax to United States phone numbers for just $0.99 every 5 pages you send.

Day One ($4.99)

Day One is great for those who are looking to start and maintain a small scale blog. While other sites like Wordpress and Blogspot are powerful and come with tons of great features, sometimes they are simply too cluttered and complex to just pick up and write as inspiration comes. Day One provides the same flexibility and power as the biggest blogging platforms, but in a clean, distraction-free setting. Instead of posting long winded blog entries, One Day is best for short, diary-like entries that are quick and to the point. Adding images is extremely easy, and you can create a passcode to prevent everyone from viewing your material. Entries can be shared privately through email as a PDF, HTML or Plain Text format, but if you'd like to start a blogging website you can use Day One's platform called Publish.

Fantastical 2 ($4.99)

If you love how the iPhone 6 and 6 Plus calendar looks on the larger screens but wish it had just a few more features, Fantastical 2 might be just what you are looking for. The biggest different between the stock iPhone calendar and Fantastical 2 is the layout - Fantastical 2 specializes in providing a highly detailed daily and weekly view, while the iPhone calendar provides more general views of days, weeks, or months. Creating an event is extremely easy, too. You can start your sentences with either reminder, todo, task, or remind me to, followed by the appointment or event, and it will automatically create the event, set a reminder, and tie everything together more reliably. Instead of filling in 4 or 5 different text fields with every event, just type in "todo get haircut tomorrow at 2pm" or "alarm 6am" and the rest is done for you.

NOAA Hi-Def Radar ($1.99)

The NOAA Hi-Def Radar will make you feel like a weather anchor. Enjoy real-time weather updates and visually see the weather patterns on a colorful radar. The app even lets you track hurricanes and lightning strikes in real time, and warnings for severe weather, wildfires, heavy snow, and storms. The latest updates bring about very consistent look and feel. Zoom in or out without experiencing loading delays or lag, and set the loop speed of the weather patterns as slow or as fast as you'd like. If you are only interested in checking the weather for a few specific places instead of a general large scale overview, you can save favorite places and skip to those instead of having to find them every time you log in.

Appendix B: Best 20 Free Apps

Dropbox

Dropbox is a great alternative or supplement to iCloud Drive. It works much the same way – you are allocated a certain amount of memory, and you can store your files on it. The biggest difference between iCloud Drive and Dropbox however is the functionality. Dropbox can be accessed through any browser or device whether it's on Android, iOS, PC, Mac, Windows phones, and anything else that can access the internet. Text editors, document viewers, and even a photo editor is included to give you powerful tools out of the box. Text links are generated for each file if you wish to share it with someone, so instead of figuring out how to email someone a 2 hour long video or want to send several zip files, you can just text or email links to each file. This will take up much less data, and you can send it through many more channels. You get 2 GB free when you sign up, and can get up to 50 GB of free storage if you take advantage of promotions they have from time to time, and they offer paid subscriptions as well for much more data, similar to iCloud Drive.

SwiftKey

SwiftKey Keyboard, one of Swype's biggest rivals, is loved by many for its powerful typing adaptation, customization, and ease of use. Much like Swype and Apple's new keyboard, SwiftKey learns your writing style and adapts to provide you with much more relevant suggestions. If you frequently type in LOL instead of lol, you will find that LOL will soon become the default. SwiftKey also has a typing mechanic that allows you to slide your finger across letters and it will spell out the words for you instead of having to tap each individual letter. With the newest update you can now sync SwiftKey with your Facebook or Gmail accounts to give it a better idea of how you type, for even more predictability. Last but certainly not least, you can customize the look and feel of the keyboard to how you see fit. Want a rainbow theme to wrap around the entire keyboard? Prefer a darker look with brighter keys? There are countless themes out there for SwiftKey, further adding to the attraction of this wonderful keyboard.

Mailbox

Inbox Zero is a state of being coveted by many professionals and smartphone users where your inbox finally reaches 0 messages, and stays that way. Many claim it to be must less stressful, more productive, and easier to manage. The makers of Dropbox bring you Mailbox, an app they believe is key to bringing everyone to that mystical Inbox Zero. Designed to make your email come and go quickly and easily, the swipe and gesture based layout will be reminiscent of iOS 7 and 8. You are able to organize mail into different categories, archive them, or trash them immediately as they come in. If something comes in but you are not ready to read it or reply to it, you can set it to come in again at a time you will check it instead of letting it accumulate in your inbox. Options for delay include later today, tomorrow, someday (for unimportant messages), and dates you can set yourself. Like Dropbox, the app is beautiful, clean, elegant, and very easy to use. A must have for the busy emailer!

Evernote

Evernote is an extremely popular productivity app that enables users to create, organize, sync, search, and share notes. If you have an idea or need to jot down a quick note to refer to later, Evernote makes it very easy to add new notes or update currently existing notes. You can organize notes into notebooks to maintain different types of notes without ending up with the equivalent of a bunch of Post-It Notes on the fridge. Some example notebooks could include diets, recipe ideas, workout routines, noteworthy news clips or videos, images you can put a story to, business ideas, just to name a few. The notes are not just limited to plain text, either. You can handwrite notes and sketches using the Penultimate add on, edit photos in the powerful Skitch add on, or add other types of notes such as business cards, voice or audio notes, and web pages. Just like with Dropbox and other competitive cloud services, you can access Evernote not just on your iPhone, but on a Mac, PC, Android phone, or most other devices.

Mint

One of the hottest startups in recent memory, Mint was quickly snatched up by finance giant Intuit, the makers of Quickbooks and Quicken. Mint is a totally free, comprehensive personal finance tracker. You can safely add all of your financial institutions, credit cards, auto and home loans, and several other types of accounts on the webpage. Once everything is added and your profile is completed, you can quite literally take a step back and view your finances in all of their entirety with just a glance. This is a wonderful way to track your spending habits, view how much money goes where, and even create budgets and goals to help you save for the things that matter most. The iPhone version is the only one to also offer a free credit score and understand what everything means on it. With such sensitive information, Mint understands the need to keep things secure. Everything is stored safely in the cloud, and account numbers are not stored on the phone.

Stocktouch

You don't have to be a professional day trader to enjoy Stocktouch and reap the benefits of a powerful, highly organized ticker application. The free version is only 5 minutes behind, but you can upgrade to the Pro version to take advantage of real time updates. The biggest draw of Stocktouch is how it utilizes data visualization in an easy to understand manner. The interface is simple and clean, and the app feels extremely fluid with no lag. On one screen you can see 9 sectors covering over 5 thousand companies, as well as thousands of news stores. With the sheer amount of information presented on these screens, you won't need another trading app. The colors are easy to digest, and many leave this app running for hours just to get a pulse on the stock market.

Wunderlist

Wunderlist has been featured in many of the best technology sites including TechCrunch, the Verge, and the New York Times, and won the 2013 Mac App of the Year. It's also used by millions of people all over the world. What makes Wunderlist so attractive is how simple the design and layout are, but how powerful the features can really become. You are able to create lists that can be accessed by friends and family (if you wish) over phones, tablets, and computers, and it's this social aspect that really stands out. Say for example you have a grocery list set up, and your partner looks it over one last time but realizes you forgot to add the milk but you're already on your way to the market - they can just update it on their end and by the time you get to the store, your list will be updated as well to reflect the changes. As an added bonus, this app looks absolutely beautiful on the new iPhone screens.

Duolingo

Duolingo is, simply put, the best way to learn a new language absolutely free. You can choose between several common languages: Spanish, Portuguese, French, German, Italian, and even English. Each language is broken down into many tiny categories and games that you can practice and progress through. Some categories include Basics 1 and 2, Phrases, Food, Animals, and Plurals. Completing each part will give you a chance to earn experience points called Lingots, causing you to level up, which in turn unlocks new categories and bonus quizzes. You are able to display your progress and skills to friends, opening you up for friendly competition.

Alien Blue

If you find yourself constantly visiting the popular forum website Reddit, Alien Blue is the perfect app for you. The developers point out that the app was created from the ground up, making for a more intuitive touchscreen experience. You will be able to easily navigate through threads and images. If you see something you like, you can click on the star icon in the upper right corner to add that thread or comment to your favorites.

Instagram

The popular photo sharing app looks better than ever on your new iPhone's higher resolution. If you don't already have this app, download it and you'll see why more than 200 million users are constantly taking and sharing photos on Instagram. The custom designed filters look great on the phone's newly upgrade camera, and you are allowed unlimited uploads with no restriction on image size. Post your photos for others to see, comment on, and follow you, or search for images and favorite photographers to follow them and stay up to date on their latest uploads. Images can be uploaded to all of the major social networks including Facebook, Twitter, Tumblr, and Flickr.

Snapchat

Snapchat is one of the hottest, fastest growing apps today. Create a message, take a picture or video, add a caption, and then send it to a friend using Snapchat's extremely light, quick program. Once your friend receives the "Snap", whatever you sent over will expire after a certain period of time elapses, which you can edit before sending anything over. This is a great way to have quick conversations or send funny photos without worrying about keeping a history of everything, and your inbox will look less cluttered. Snapchat is all about real time conversations and media exchanges, so you'll be able to see when a friend is typing to you, and vice versa. You will also be able to tell when they have received or viewed your Snaps and Chats.

Facebook

Arguably the biggest social networking site in the world, Facebook boasts over 1.28 billion (yes, billion) active monthly users. The iPhone app is optimized to keep you up to date on all of your friends most important status updates, while letting you keep in touch with friends and relatives through comments, messages, and shared links. With the iPhone app you are able to upload a picture or video immediately after taking it, create and upload status updates on the fly, get notified any time you get a photo, video, or status liked or commented on, and use your favorite apps.

If you are not on an unlimited data plan, be sure to switch Facebook's video auto play to Off or Wi-Fi Only. By default it's set to On, which means that while scrolling through your news feed, all of those videos will begin to play in their entirety whether you are watching them or not. This has caused a lot of background data consumption for users. To change this setting, go to your iPhone's Settings menu, scroll down to Facebook, and click on Settings again. Click on Auto-Play and select either Wi-Fi Only or Off, and then back out of the settings menu.

Pinterest

Pinterest is another app that looks amazing on the larger iPhone screens. The layout has been redesigned to show you much more information while looking even less cluttered, and the landscape mode on the iPhone 6 Plus makes Pinterest look as if it were being displayed on an iPad. If you haven't heard of Pinterest, basically it's a scrapbooking app that allows you to search and "Pin" links, articles, images, or groups that interest you. If you are looking for things like Christmas tree ideas, tattoo designs, vacations, art or Halloween decoration ideas, just search for those terms and you will be greeted with some very creative ideas, designs, and DIY projects that will keep you busy on rainy days or through the weekends. You can also create your own pins if you have a cool arts and crafts project you'd like to share, or maybe you've rearranged your living room in the most perfect way and want to share it with the world.

Lose It!

Lose It! Is one of the best apps if your goal is to lose weight or just be more healthy overall. Once the app is downloaded, just create an account and tell the app some information about yourself, then the app does the rest of the work for you. It will lay out a comprehensive plan to shed excess weight and get in shape (or stay in shape), and all you need to do is log exercise and food as you eat it. Keeping track of calories is easy, with a gigantic database of food items that include many restaurants, as well as a barcode scanner if you need to scan in a particular food or snack. Lose It! also has great third party functionality. If you own a Bluetooth enabled health wristband such as the Jawbone Up, or a Wi-Fi connected scale such as the Fitbit Aria Body Scale, the app will be able to connect and sync with those devices, ensuring your health is being carefully monitored across several different platforms.

MyFitnessPal

MyFitnessPal is similar to Lose It, but with more of an emphasis on tracking the food you eat, if you can believe it. The food database is the largest on any iOS calorie counter program with over 4 million different foods. It tracks exercise as well, but not as strongly as other fitness apps like Lose It or JEFIT Pro. The emphasis here is definitely on calorie counting – you can enter meals by searching keywords, scanning barcodes, and creating your own custom foods. You can also save entire meals, so if you have a favorite meal such as chicken stir fry with brown rice, you can save it as one item instead of having to type in each item separately every time you eat it. With the introduction of iOS 8, MyFitnessPal integrates perfectly with Apple Health, syncing your weight, tracking your steps, and adding your meal summaries for easy viewing.

My Net Diary

Another high quality fitness app is My Net Diary, which calculates your target calories based on important factors such as your age, weight, height, and gender. Sporting almost 600,000 unique foods, the food database here is also quite robust, though nowhere near as large as MyFitnessPal. You can easily create, edit, or search for foods to count calories, but other functions include tracking calories burned through exercising, keeping tabs on how much water and vitamins you are taking in, and logging measurements of your body so you can really see your progress. One of the coolest features of this app is the many different serving sizes you can choose for a food. If you select even a banana, it will give you several different options including small, medium, large, or extra large, each with their own corresponding nutrients.

RunKeeper

If you aren't a fan of gyms but have a competitive spirit and love to run, jog, or cycle, RunKeeper is the app for you. The app takes advantage of the iPhone's highly accurate GPS to track your running pace, cycling speed, route distance, and efficiency. You will be able to view your route on the map, charted out and showing you areas of improvement. Whether you are training for a marathon or just want to get in shape, the sheer amount of data displayed based on your run or bike session will keep you wanting to improve yourself on many different levels. If you are a beginner, there are many different running and walking plans to choose from that will get you distance running in no time, and if you are bored of a particular route, viewing other runners' routes and saving them can breathe some fresh air on your routine. Like other health and fitness apps, RunKeeper can synchronize and work together with your other health tracking devices like the FitBit, Pebble smartwatch or Garmin Forerunner GPS Watches to really monitor your vitals accurately.

Chrome

If the iPhone's native web browsing app Safari is not doing enough for you, perhaps Google Chrome is what you need. If you already use Chrome on your Mac or PC, all you need to do is log into your Gmail account for all of your bookmarks, history, and web pages to sync up on your iPhone. This app prides itself on speed, and you will notice no lag while switching seamlessly between several different tabs and searching for multiple things at once. The incognito mode works a little better than Safari's private browsing since you don't need to close all tabs when making the change, and the small user interface avoids distracting the user from browsing the web. Overall, Chrome provides a clean interface with a very light design that lets you enjoy the web without having to fuss over the smaller details.

Onavo Extend

If you are on a limited data plan but love to spend time on your iPhone away from Wi-Fi,

Onavo Extend will help you enjoy using your phone without having to worry about using up all of your data and constantly having to keep track of your usage. It's designed to run in the background any time you are not connected to a Wi-Fi network, but shuts itself off as soon as it detects a stable internet connection. Onavo Extend works by compressing data into much smaller pieces that come in just as quick with no notable lag, while using a lot less data. Whether it's audio, video, text messages, or internet browsing, this app will let you do more of what you love without the potentially expensive data drain.

AllRecipes Dinner Spinner

Here's another app that looks wonderful on the extra iPhone screen real estate. AllRecipes Dinner Spinner is an app made by the popular cooking and recipe website AllRecipes. The app taps into the website's database of over 30 million users and the custom recipes they've created to share with everyone else. You can search for that special recipe by specifying which ingredients you already have (or want to use), and which ingredients you want to omit. You can also select any special nutritional needs you may have and sort by cooking time so you find exactly what you'd be interested in. There are also seasonal recipes, and if you have a dish you like to cook, recipes can be typed in and uploaded to be viewed, shared, reviewed, and discussed by other users. Best of all, there is a built in Recipe Box that allows you to quickly and easily store favorite recipes you may stumble upon. The iPhone version also comes with an exclusive feature: just shake your phone and a random recipe will pop up, making this a great tool to use when you're out of ideas for dinner.

GrubHub

An app that's been seeing more media coverage lately, GrubHub is an app that basically lets you order delivery or pickup from many different restaurants. The benefit of using GrubHub over just browsing search engines for restaurant menus and ordering online though their website is that GrubHub shows you many different restaurants for whichever particular style of food you are craving. These restaurants all display reviews, menus, and other restaurant information to help you make a decision. GrubHub shines in its payment abilities. Regardless of what the restaurant you are ordering from accepts, using GrubHub will allow you to pay using cash, credit, and even PayPal. The app also lets you store credit card or PayPal information to make the next transaction quicker. There is no fee whatsoever for GrubHub users, so if you find yourself ordering takeout or delivery often, this is definitely an app worth trying at least a few times.

CNN

Among the countless different news apps, CNN stands out as one of the most gorgeous looking programs. On the higher resolution screens, this app will look like the iPad version, which resembles a sort of digital newspaper the way it's laid out and arranged. News articles will update in real time, breaking news stories will be prominently displayed in a banner at the very top of the screen. The images and text look crisp on the iPhone display, and videos look great. Depending on the cable provider, live coverage can also be enjoyed. You can also enable notifications so that important news stories or those relevant to your interests will always come flowing in.

Airbnb

Traveling has never been so fun. Originally called Air Bed and Breakfast, Airbnb was created in 2008 and has seen exponential growth since then. It was designed to allow travelers a way to find lodging for high profile events where hotels were too busy to book, but has developed into a channel where all kinds of travelers can stay at privately owned properties in over 190 countries at great prices. You can search for properties by location, and once you find a favorite spot, can get in touch with that property's owner to confirm your stay and iron out the payment details. The choices for stay are not limited to just rooms – you can rent out entire houses, apartments, boathouses, shacks, attics, and even castles or igloos.

Viber

Here's another great app for travelers, or those who have friends and family living in or frequently visiting other countries. Calling, texting, and communicating in general with people living outside of the country you are in can get quite expensive. Viber has focused on this pain point and the result is a reliable app that you can use to text, call, and even send media messages to other people, regardless of where in the world they are and what kind of phone they have. All you need is a 3G, 4G LTE, or Wi-Fi connection and a valid phone number already. Viber links up to your phone number so others can find you and vice versa, and that's it! Like Snapchat, you will also be able to see when messages are received or read through the read receipt function, and you can also tell when the other party is typing.

Skype

Originally called Sky Peer to Peer, Skype is perhaps the most well-known video communication program today. Owned by Microsoft since 2011, Skype is available on all platforms and is loved for its ease of use when it comes to creating and maintaining contact lists, sending or receiving files, and connecting with others. The service provides free instant messaging to other Skype users in addition to the video chats. You can also call other Skype users like a regular phone call, but calls to those who do not have Skype will be charged. While Skype might seem pointless since your iPhone has FaceTime, this is a good alternative for when you'd like to communicate through video or instant messaging with loved ones who might not have an Apple product capable of using FaceTime.

Conclusion

The launch of the latest iPhone models brought with them many new changes to the operating system through iOS 8, and through the hardware itself. It may seem like there is so much to learn, but with the help of this guide you should now be more familiarized and able to thoroughly enjoy your phone without feeling frustrated. The 50 apps we've picked out for you will keep you busy for a long time, and your iPhone will demonstrate how much more it can do besides make calls and keep you connected with those closest to you.

Printed in Great Britain
by Amazon

47446417R00041